Spinks & Ouzels

Christmas Poems by Mark DeBolt

Spinks and Ouzels sing sublimely,
"We too have a Savior born."
~Christopher Smart

spink=finch — *ouzel=blackbird*

holy fool press

Contact:
Mark DeBolt
30 W Park Ave
Apt 211
Coldwater MI 49036
onionjuice@cbpu.com

*for all my family & friends
especially Debbie Dally*

Preface

This book contains all the Christmas poems I wrote before Christmas 1913 which I still consider worthy of keeping, and which were not included in *A Wreath of Twisted Thorn*, *This Mystery I Pose*, or *The Christmas Hymns of Mark DeBolt*. Most of these poems have appeared in various chapbooks or were distributed privately for various past Christmases.

The main body of this book is miscellaneous Christmas poems arranged in alphabetical order. There are also two appendices containing poems that did not seem appropriate for this treatment. The first of these consists of parodies on poems by Lewis Carroll. The second consists of renderings of carols from various Celtic languages. They are fairly literal to the original meanings and may be sung to the original tunes. You might note that the meter is sometimes quite rough, but this is true of the originals as well.

My hope for this book is that it will bless you, and add beauty and meaning to your celebration of the Christmas season.

Merry Messiahmas!
MD

Absolutely Empty

The child angels, with clothes hanger wings
from the balcony announced and sang
a baby dolly lying in a manger.

The child shepherds in their bathrobes came
down the aisle with their walking sticks
and children dressed like impressionist sheep.

The children left. The angels went away.
A star appeared, projected from a spotlight
on the balcony where the angels had been.

The child wise men in their cotton beards
and graduation gowns came down the aisle
bearing containers absolutely empty

of gold and frankincense and myrrh—the gifts
they were to give to the baby dolly—
they were to give to Jesus Christ our Lord.

The containers were absolutely empty.
And Jesus, I, when I give you my heart,
give a container absolutely empty.

And See This Thing

In Islamic tradition, Gabriel had 280 wings.

Two hundred eighty wings, and wonderful
the way they flutter, the way they fold in prayer
before the throne of thunder; aureole
that takes its color from a violent star

in the East, rainbow-twinkling, moonbeam-bright;
dripping from golden hair a golden rain;—
some see it so and others see it not—
the painting's painted but the colors run.

Gabriel Angelo, the strength of God;
Gabriel Angelo, vanguard of grief,
that promised Mary, though she be a maid,
a shadow o'er her, through her soul a knife—

this is the messenger of martyrdom
that shocked the shepherds with the command, "Come!"

Annunciation

Gabriel greets in her garden the Graceful:
"The prince of all pieces now patents you peaceful,

with peace that partakes of the pattern of passion,
the movement of madness, the music of motion.

Woman, in your womb a whirlwind wakens,
the quivering quake of a cataract quickens.

Maiden, you'll mother the motionless mover,
for God is the gift and his Ghost is the giver.

A boy shall be born who obeys the Bible,
though stuck in a stall and stranded in a stable.

Next they will nail him whose nest is so narrow.
Your soul shall be sundered with the sword of sorrow.

He shall defeat darkness, death and the devil.
His ground shall be grace and his grave be mere gravel.

Lady, your lad shall be your lord and lover,
for God is the gift and his Ghost is the giver."

As I Lay Dying

As I lay dying, who was singing?
All the servants in my golden hall
  raised their voice in loud thanksgiving
as I lay dying in a cattle stall.
  I was too dumb to say, "I am
    too dumb to speak at all,"
  as I lay dying in Bedlam
    in a cattle stall.

As I lay dying, who was shining?
A bright celestial creature gave off
  the final measure of his burning
as I lay dying in a feeding trough.
  I was too dull to say, "I am."
    I could but cry and cough
  as I lay dying in Bedlam
    in a feeding trough.

As I lay dying, who was watching?
Bedlam bumpkins clad in burlap bags
  stood around awkwardly gawking
as I lay dying in torn linen rags.
  I was too sick to say, "I am
    sick of the cloth that gags,"
  as I lay dying in Bedlam
    in torn linen rags.

As I lay dying, who was coming?
Three wealthy pagan priests who read
  the stars for kings were hurrying
as I lay dying in the cattle feed.
  I was too young to say, "I am."
    I could but weep and bleed
  as I lay dying in Bedlam
    in the cattle feed.

The Black Madonna

There are a number of very old European icons which show Mary &
the baby Jesus with very dark skin. This representation is known as
"the Black Madonna".

Her skin is dark.
And was it so?
I do not know
the shade—the birch's or oak's bark.

Her skin is black.
And was it thus?
She's each of us
who mother God in our heart's shack.

Our every shade—
the dark and light,
black, red, brown, white,
yellow, olive—were in that maid.

Give birth to Christ
and join with her.
The shade of her
is your own shade. Give birth to Christ.

Carol: a Satire

On Yule Night, on Yule Night,
   now worship we the sun,
and call him forth with fires bright
   and orgiastic fun.

On Wassail Night, on Wassail Night
   now worship we the ale,
which spins our heads, makes our eyes bright—
   we drink it by the pail.

On Christmas Night, on Christmas Night
   now worship we the Christ,
with tunes too quaint and lights too bright
   and presents overpriced.

Carol: a Silence

(here ends the poem)

Child, Child

In an orient stable's crib,
removed from your mother's rib,
child, child, how still you lie!

In an orient inn's neglect,
known too little to reject,
child, child, how nil you lie.

In an orient garden's tomb,
as if in a wounded womb,
child, child, how will you lie?

The Child in the Chalice

Sir Gawain's Vision

The child in the chalice
  once walked a golden street
and lived within a palace
  haunted by Paraclete.

The child in the chalice
  where God and mortal meet
will soon be met with malice
  of men and know defeat.

The child in the chalice
  was born of common wheat:
I don't wish to seem callous
  but he is good to eat.

Christ-&-Go-Seek

Strike the harp and join the jolly,
Christ is hid behind the holly.

Strike the harp and whet the whistle,
Christ is hid beneath the mistle.

Strike the harp and deal the deuces,
Christ is hid between the spruces.

Strike the harp and turn the table.
Christ is hid within the stable.

Strike the harp and dare the danger,
Christ is hid without the manger.

Christmas Poem for Merideth

16 years after

Merideth, wherever
you are (and I am sure
you do not want me there)
I ask you, remember
me in your Christmas prayer;
for thoughts of what you were
before betrayal are
the gifts I'm grateful for:
they hurt—the hurt is pure.

Christus Natus Est, Noel!

(Christ is born. Noel!)

Christmas comes and the geese fatten.
Paper angels sing in Latin.
I say "sing"—they really spell:
"Christus natus est. Noel!"

On the tree the decorations
symbolize anticipations.
What we wish we'll never tell.
Christus natus est. Noel!

From the kitchen an aroma
teases twice as much as soma.
Oh to hear the dinner bell!
Christus natus est. Noel!

But we'll have church before dinner.
God, make a saint of this sinner.
God, make heaven of my hell.
Christus natus est. Noel!

A Crib of Corn

No cradle but a crib of corn.
The wool that from the sheep was shorn
provided him something to wear
to keep him warm. A single tear
fell from his mother's eye when he
screamed and wailed and wept, for she
did not know why. Did he need changed?
Or fed? Or his bed re-arranged?
Yet all seem right. Perhaps he saw
the day he would show his meat raw,
his flesh impaled upon a stake.
Perhaps he just had a headache.
Perhaps he felt a bit forlorn—
no cradle but a crib of corn.

Dark Places

"Holy places are dark places."
   ~C. S. Lewis

Dark was the womb from which the Light
of Lights came forth in a dark stall
   upon the darkest night
          of all.
Holy places are dark places.

Dark were the bands that bound his beams.
Dark was the trough in which he slept,
   where lost in darkest dreams
          he wept.
Holy places are dark places.

His dark heart burned with a dark flame,
and darkness filled his infant mind.
   The souls to whom he came
          were blind.
Holy places are dark places.

O Savior, enter my dark heart.
Dwell in the darkness of my brain.
   Say to my soul, "Thou art
          my fane."
Holy places are dark places.

Say to my soul, "Thou art the womb
in which I am knit and made whole.
   My temple is thy tomb,
          O soul.
Holy places are dark places."

Emmanuel

"Emmanuel" she named him,
  but did not tell the name.
The angel called him "Jesus."
  —The two must be the same.

The moment that she claimed him
  she gave it all away.
He's the Almighty. He's us.
  Salvation is the pay.

The Fourteen Kingdoms
on the Coming of the Illuminator

after a poem in "The Revelation of Adam"
an ancient Coptic writing from the Nag Hammadi library

The first kingdom says of him:
He came from the nameless source.
He came as a spirit to heaven.
He came to the bosom of his mother.
He was nourished.
He received glory and power.
And thus he came to the water.

The second kingdom says of him:
He came from a great prophet.
A bird carried the newborn child to a high mountain.
An angel came and said to him, "Arise, God has given you glory."
He was nourished by the bird of heaven.
He received glory and power.
And thus he came to the water.

The third kingdom says of him:
He came from a virgin which Solomon had sought with all his
      armies.
She was not what Solomon expected.
The virgin conceived and gave birth to the child.
He was nourished by her on the edge of the desert and received
      from the seed which begot him.
He received glory and power.
And thus he came to the water.

The sixth kingdom says of him:
He came from the world above.
The virgin gathered flowers in the world below.
She conceived from the love of the flowers and bore him.
He was nourished by the angels of the flower garden.
He received glory and power.
And thus he came to the water.

The seventh kingdom says of him:
He came as a drop from heaven to earth.
Dragons carried him down to caverns where he became a child.
A spirit came on him and took him up to where the drop had
      come from.
He was nourished.
He received glory and power.
And thus he came to the water.

The eighth kingdom says of him:
A cloud came upon the earth.
The cloud enveloped a rock.
He came forth.
He was nourished by the angels over the cloud.
He received glory and power.
And thus he came to the water.

The ninth kingdom says of him:
A muse went by herself to a high mountain and dwelt there alone.
She desired to bear a child without the aid of a man.
Her desire was fulfilled, and she conceived and bore him.
He was nourished by the angels over the desire.
He received glory and power.
And thus he came to the water.

The tenth kingdom says of him:
God loved the cloud of glory.
God begot him and cast him into the cloud which surrounds God.
He was born.
He was nourished by the cloud of glory.
He received glory and power.
And thus he came to the water.

(continued)

The eleventh kingdom says of him:
The Father loved his daughter.
She conceived by the power of the Father.
She hid the child in a desert tomb.
He was nourished by the angel.
He received glory and power.
And thus he came to the water.

The twelfth kingdom says of him:
He came from the sun.
He came from the moon.
He came from all the stars.
He was nourished.
He received glory and power.
And thus he came to the water.

The thirteenth kingdom says of him:
The King is continually born as the Word.
He received form.
He was provided for.
He was nourished.
He received glory and power.
And thus he came to the water.

The kingless kingdom says of him:
God chose him from all ages.
God gave him the knowledge of pure truth.
God said, "From the world of worlds the Light has come forth."
He nourished his chosen people.
He received glory and power.
And thus he came to the water.

Halos

What was he thinking, the painter, giving
   halo to least and greatest beast,
sheep and camel and all those then living
      in haloed stall?

Halo too to messenger and human,
   foolish and wise and of the skies.
The brightest halo give to the woman
      who made God live

as one of us. Yet God is not haloed,
   who is made meat mid haloed wheat
and haloed clichéd vine. Only hallowed
      head does not shine.

Hallelujahweh!

Hallelujahweh!
  Jesus is born.
Follow him alway,
  though stretched and torn.

After his stretching
  he shall arise,
life from hell fetching,
  fooling the wise.

After his tearing,
  no tear shall fall,
for he is bearing
  life for us all.

Follow him alway,
  tonight, tomorn.
Hallelujahweh!
  Jesus is born.

Holier than High Heaven

Holier than high heaven,
  the harrower of hell
is cornered in a corn crib,
  a captive crownless king.
  Celestial servants sing
songs sorrowful times seven:
  in tattered tunes they tell
a trap tricks in the torn crib.

The pearl pure and priceless,
  the prince and priest of peace,
is stationed in a stable,
  a straw stall his estate.
  A maiden without mate
no mansion mold- or mice-less
  can let, have lent, or lease.
She leaves her lad a label

on brow and bosom branded
  of a bum born midst beasts.
The wicked wormy world
  has won his wondrous wealth
  by stunt and scheme and stealth.
But still the stable-stranded
  has prosperous prophet-priests
provide perfume plush-pearled.

Ich Am of Northpole

a parody of "Ich am of Ireland"

   Ich am of Northpole
and of the holy pole
     of Northpole.
Sire, be good because
if thee break any laws
Ile tell saint Nicholas
     in Northpole.

Interior Cradle

Three astrologer-priests disguised as kings
knelt down before the cradle in my heart.
(Ignore the form that on the crosstree hangs.
Ignore the dicing for the hanged man's shirt.)

Three advisors disguised as messengers
knelt down before the cradle in my nerves.
(Ignore the consummation of all fears.
Ignore the flesh the legal weapon carves.)

Three diviner-sages disguised as saints
knelt down before the cradle in my mind.
(Ignore the wounds, the many bloody fonts.
Ignore the flood where blood and water blend.)

Three individuals revealed as all
knelt down before the Jesus in my soul.

It Out-Herods Herod

"Within a humble barn
        is born
a knave child," he said
        and sighed.
"Who needs another brat?"
        But bright
above to make him stare
        a star
announced the newborn boy
        baby,
and some heard angels sing
        a song
of glory brought to pass
        and peace
with the newborn as *how*.
        But who
was blind and deaf? He sighed
        and said,
"Better someone should knive
        the knave."

The London Zoo

If I could go
anywhere on
Christmas Eve, I'd
choose the London

Zoo. They say all
animals kneel
at midnight on
Christmas Eve. The

camels kneel. The
elephants kneel.
The penguins and
the peacocks kneel.

I would like to
see a giraffe
kneel—just once. I'd
like to see a

jackrabbit kneel.
I would really
like to see a
snake kneel. How can

a snake kneel when
he doesn't have
any legs, let
alone knees? They

say he's evil.
Perhaps he is
the only one
that doesn't kneel.

But then again,
perhaps he finds
a way to kneel—
he's so clever.

Love Song from a Chimney

It's dark in here, and sooty. As I put
on weight each year, it grows a tighter squeeze.
I wriggle my way down, suck in my gut.
I guess that I'd do anything to please.
I guess that that makes me some kind of nut.
I don't do it for show. Nobody sees
my annual descent down this chute, but
she knows I do it. She's left me cookies

as always, and I'm grateful, though it's small
reward for climbing down this ashy hole.
She sleeps in her bedroom, just down the hall,
where all my thoughts are with her. But my role
does not allow a peek at her. They call
me a saint for the presents that I dole
out each year—for her alone, but to all—
before returning to the frozen pole.

Mad Song after Midnight Mass

a sacred parody of "Changeling" by Leah Bodine Drake

I am out in the chill of a still midnight.
I have drunk sacred blood in a mystic rite,
and the alcheme wine has invaded each vein
as the burning of incense infested my brain.
Now I chant "hoc est corpus" through the freezing rain,
for the sane is insane and the insane is sane.
       Mad I be.
       Mad I be
    when the blessed blood runs red in me.

I have followed the street as the sleet cuts deep.
I have followed a star to where women weep.
I am lost in a labyrinthine royal hall
where the throne is a trough and the court is a stall
and the stable is decked out in purple and pall
and the babies within have been slain one and all.
       Sad I be.
       Sad I be
    when the blessed blood runs red in me.

There's a chalice whose liquor can quickly give
  fresh blood to the grave folk and make them to live.
There's a new silver bell whose glad clamor is old.
I have caroled noel as this great bell was tolled.
Though the bell was but silver, the chalice was gold
and its warmth keeps me singing noel through the cold.
       Glad I be.
       Glad I be
    when the blessed blood runs red in me.

The Magus

This darkness eats my heart. There is no star
like the voyaging ball of flame that led
three of my fellow magi to the store
of hay on which a baby king was laid.

I did not go with them. I had the state
to tend to, and I really thought I could
track the star latter if I was astute.
Now I would go, but the trail has grown cold.

My fellow magi have returned to tell
how the king that they found has surely fled
a tyrant's wrath and must stay hid until
the tyrant dies. My eyes create a flood

for what I've missed. The flood waters a plant
that bears a bud. The bud becomes a bloom,
a sexless blossom of my dark complaint,
a flower of my anguish and self-blame.

A bitter hope grows in a barren cup.
If I follow this darkness I might find
the secret that my fellow magi keep,
the heart that beats within the king they found.

A Maiden in Her Garden

A maiden in her garden prayed,
was startled by a brilliancy
that moved and spoke as if human.
The brilliancy told her that she
   was not to be afraid,
for she would mother God the Son.
   Surely that day had more
  delight than any other
   that God had known before,
  for God now had a mother.

The magi left their ancient school
of secret wisdom in the East
to seek him whom a star proclaimed.
They found a babe housed like a beast,
   for wisdom played the fool
when the unnameable was named.
   Surely that day had more
  madness than any hatter—
   mystery bared its core,
  for mind had become matter.

A tetrarch heard about this boy,
conceived a threat to crown and throne.
He ordered many babies dead
to ensure that one death alone,
   but he did not destroy
  the boy who to the desert fled.
   Surely that day had more
  humility and meekness
   than any day before,
  for God now had a weakness.

Mary the Maiden at the Annunciation

Mary the maiden rocked
with fear, although the angel said,
    "Fear not!",
although the pure angelical
  to the angelbeast bowed.

Mary the maiden thought
it must be some celestial joke.
    No flaw
in her? She knew her flaws too well—
  yet none for her own sake.

Mary the maiden said
she would do what the Lord would have her do,
    though it
should prove to be impossible—
  but God does all, and so

Mary the maiden gave
humanity to the divine,
    thus made
the pure unimaginable
  and the pure image one.

Merry Christmas, Merideth

Merry Christmas, Merideth.
Many happy New Years after.
  May your Noels make your breath
    vibrate with laughter.

  May the fat saint bring to you
what you wish, not what you ask for,
  kindly finding no fault to
    bring you to task for.

  Kindness, blindness—much the same
in this valley of deceiving,
  in this wilderness of shame,
    this grove of grieving.

  Here I wish for you a very
happy life and a merry death.
  And have a very merry
    Christmas, Merideth.

Noel Kyrie

For those who can-
not hear or see
the angels chant,
Lord, have mercy.

That the fat man
might laugh when we
refuse his grant,
Lord, have mercy.

For those who plan
their family
and those who can't,
Lord, have mercy.

For misers in
their misery,
for scrooge and grinch,
Christ, have mercy.

When friends and kin
give miles and we
take but an inch,
Christ, have mercy.

For those who grin
incessantly
and never flinch,
Christ, have mercy.

For presents un-
derneath the tree
that we don't want,
Lord, have mercy.

That anyone
might hear when we
a thank-you grunt,
Lord, have mercy.

For those whose fun
lacks mystery,
whose joy is blunt,
Lord, have mercy.

An Old Bell Re-rung

Christmas comes.
Geese get fat.
Put two cents
in my hat.
No two cents?
One will do.
Not a cent?
God bless you!

On a Theme from Christopher Smart

Spinks and ouzels sing sublimely, "We too
have a savior born," for Messiah brought
his grace not solely for humanity,
but for each bird and fish and bug and brute.

All fauna co-inherited the fall
from one fell fruit, though Adam was to blame.
All fauna was de-natured through one fell
demon-snake. Spink and ouzels sing sublime-

ly, "We too have a savior born." O snake,
join now the chorus of the joyful song!
Be devil-snake no more with poison-snack.
Be angel-snake. With spinks and ouzels sing

sublimely, "We too have a savior born."
Too, fruit and flower and weed and wood to burn.

On the Wings of the Storm

"And dark is his path on the wings of the storm."
~Robert Grant, "O Worship the King"

No one wants cloud
on Christmas Eve;
but morning comes, it lauds as loud
as sinners who believe.

The airs declare
what lightning splits.
No angel on gold thoroughfare
flutters or floats or flits.

Still in a stall
an infant sleeps,
and the universe is too small
to clasp the dream he keeps.

His gracious wrath
will keep us warm.
Dark is his visionary path
on the wings of the storm.

No one wants rain
on Christmas Day,
but down it comes and leaves a stain
Christ's blood must wash away.

The Peer & the Poor

The peer
and the poor,
  with cheer
in their chore,
seek out the poorer quarters where
  the ragged people go.

The lord
of the lash,
  the hoard-
er of trash,
with what presents they can afford,
  genuflect in the snow

in front
of the need
  and want
of a feed
trough used as a bed. To be blunt,
  it's not much of a show.

How odd
that they seek
  the quad
of the meek!
And yet it is there they find God
  in the Highest below.

Rachel Weeps

Rachel weeps and rejects comfort.
  Rachel weeps in anguished pain,
for the king who fears and trembles
  sought the king who came to reign,
sought him not to bow and worship
  but to slay him by the sword.
He has slain a hundred infants,
  but has not slain Christ the Lord.

Rachel weeps for her dead children,
  weeps and won't be comforted.
Rachel weeps in endless sorrow,
  for her children are all dead.
But her children weep no longer,
  no more sigh and no more frown,
for her children are in heaven,
  each one wears a martyr's crown.

The Season's Risk

Sometimes you hear rumors, reports even,
someone killed by a falling icycle.
[I have read (and believe it true) ten
times more people killed by coconuts fall-

ing on them than by shark attacks.] I avoid
beneathing icicles and mistletoe.
Yet sometimes through a must door there hangs overhead
something surrendering the season's joy;

and what am I to do but risk my life
by this frozen sharpness? to risk my mind
by the melty softness of those lips? If
I die or fall in love, please understand

it is the season's risk, not mine by choice,
afraid of falling kisses, falling ice.

A Secret Which Surprises Us No More

a villanelle

God a newborn behind a stable door
came unexpected to a doubting age,
a secret which surprises us no more.

An angel first announced it to the poor,
a star first portended it to the mage,
God a newborn behind a stable door.

Though few indeed were told that heavenly lore,
his birthday now is all the yearly rage,
a secret which surprises us no more.

Ignorant then, we now choose to ignore
or not ignore, engage or not engage
God a newborn behind a stable door.

It is a much too often used trapdoor
causing a disappearance from the stage,
a secret which surprises us no more;

it is the seed inside the apple core;
it is a re-read mystery's last page—
God a newborn behind a stable door,
a secret which surprises us no more.

Sir Clarrus' Carol

I'm getting awful hungry, but
King Arthur will not let us eat
until a marvel has occurred,
and so I keep my Christmas fast.

Marvels are rare enough these days.
Though I remember when they were
daily events, it's not so now,
and so I keep my Christmas fast.

If Merlin were around he would
make some marvel so we could chow,
but Merlin has been long since bound,
and so I keep my Christmas fast.

I wonder, could I engineer
some trick that would pass muster with
King Arthur? But I don't know how,
and so I keep my Christmas fast.

The sun is setting, winter's night
comes on and the feast is stone cold,
but Arthur made this silly vow,
and so I keep my Christmas fast.

Song of Simeon

"Love is like the lion's tooth."
  ~William Butler Yeats

God himself in flesh disguising
  you shall love with maiden's love,
  you shall love with mother's love.
Rising falling—falling rising;
  and the sword shall pierce you both.
  Love is like the lion's tooth.

God himself in flesh revealing
  you would with your soul protect,
  you would with your breasts protect,
near your heart safely concealing;
  but the sword shall pierce you both.
  Love is like the lion's tooth.

Song of the Virgin Mother

after a poem in "On the Origin of the World",
an ancient Coptic writing from the Nag Hammadi library

I am part of my mother.
I am the mother.
I am the wife.
I am the virgin.
I am the pregnant.
I am the midwife.
I am the comforter of birth pains.
My husband bore me.
I am his mother.
He is my strength.
He speaks reasonably of his desires.
I am becoming.
I have borne a human as Lord.

Spinks & Ouzels

Though only humans ate the fruit,
the curse was shared by bird and brute.
The frozen poles, the tepid and the torrid zones
are crowded with creaturely groans
calling in code the Lord Christ's name,
and unto them the Lord Christ came.

The citizens of tooth and claw
yearn for a more pacific law,
while those who tear nothing but green and herb and grass
pray that the time will come to pass
when prey and pounce and slaughter cease
and the Lord Christ is prince and peace.

Yearning and prayer are not in vain,
for he is born who soon shall reign
not only over humankind but over all
animals burdened by the fall,
till the last least trace of the curse
is removed from the universe.

Come, hear the carol of all fowl
from hummingbird to hooded owl.
Come, kneel with ox and cow, donkey and sheep.
The deep wild, the wild deep,
barnyard, aquarium and zoo
cry out, "We have a savior too!"

The eager jaguar, the slow sloth,
the flaccid whale, the flighty moth,
the spineless worm, the hedgehog with his spiny back,
the hart with his twelve-pointed rack,
the rhino with his single horn
sing, "We too have a savior born!"

To a Pink Advent Candle

I hesitate to light you, lest you burn
to nothing, symbol of my Advent joy.
You are a wisdom I would not unlearn.
You are a warrant I would not destroy.

And yet the season demands that I light
your wick with a wicked Lucifer match.
Your flame will mark the measure of your height
lower and lower still, till my heart catch

the fiery licks that dance as they destroy.
When will I ever learn? When will I learn
that destruction is at the root of joy?
I hesitate to light you, lest you burn.

To Out-fox a Fox

"It out-Herods Herod. Pray you, avoid it."
~William Shakespeare, "Hamlet"

Fooling is not finding; I have found
truth is never subtle, but complex.
Only those who do not understand
foxhood attempt to out-fox a fox.

It out-Herods Herod. Pray you, pray.
No it doesn't. Still stay at your prayers.
If you cannot stay at your prayers, stay
in the confidence that someone cares.

It out-Herods Herod. Yes it does.
Now always out-does what once was done.
It out Santa-Clauses Santa Claus.
Christmas is where Childermas begun.

It out-Herods Herod. So they say.
Does it? Does it? Still stay at your prayers.
If you cannot, pray that you may pray,
knowing that a living child cares.

To the Mirror, the Shadow

"The mirror of an Endless Life,
The shadow of a Virgin Wife . . ."
        ~Thomas Traherne

The chute is shut, the womb is hollow.
        The angel came
        and you became
   the mirror of an endless life,
   the shadow of a virgin wife.

First fear will lead, but love will follow.
        The spirit came
        and you became
   the mirror of an endless life,
   the shadow of a virgin wife.

Bitter the bite, but sweet the swallow.
        The baby came
        and you became
   the mirror of an endless life,
   the shadow of a virgin wife.

Unstable Stable

In an unstable stable
   most fragile God came out
his mother's womb, unable
to say what it was all about,

and yet able to keep the
   fixed stars within their course
with his word. Worship, weep the
innocent universal source

and end, just now beginning.
   He wails. The world's new
to his eyes—worth the winning
by losing—what he does, will do.

What will he do but die on
   the shadow of our shame?
What does he do but cry on,
unable to say why he came?

Upon Observing the Winter Solstice on Two Calendars

Winter begins upon Midwinter's Day—
an accident of calendars. I pray
my Winter may begin when half-way through,
      and not when new.

The Wisdom of the Wise

We went. Of course we went. We saw a star
that demanded we go. Thus we were sent
not by our monarch, but someone more high
who could write his announcements on the sky.
What could we do but go? Though it was far,
we could not choose but go, and so we went.

The star said we must go, and we obeyed.
We sought a sight that promised to astound.
We brought expensive gifts of gold and spice,
and in our wisdom thought they would suffice.
I deal in wisdom. Wisdom is my trade.
But when we got to that wee shed, I found

my wisdom was mere folly where that king
rested without a hint of majesty.
We gave our gifts (for what else could we do?),
but saw they were meaningless to that new-
born baby. We had nothing else to bring,
and were embarrassed by our poverty,

We turned and left and eventually came
to our own country, though we changed our route.
We brought with us the gifts the baby gave
to us: the greater wisdom of the knave,
the memory of our embarrassed shame,
the wondering what it was all about.

APPENDIX ONE

CARROLL PARODIES

How Doth Rudolph the Reindeer

How doth Rudolph the Reindeer
   Brighten his shining nose
Without the slightest pain, dear,
   Until it fairly glows!

How cheerful seems his famous flight,
   How neat he pierces fog,
As brilliant as the flames of light
   That burn the Yule-log!

Father Christmas

"You are old, Father Christmas," the young man said,
  "And have grown most uncommonly fat,
Yet you come down the chimney heels over head—
  Pray what is the reason for that?"

"In my youth," Father Christmas replied to the lad,
  "I used to come in by the door,
But once I got shot by a young lady's dad,
  And so I use that route no more."

"You are old, Father Christmas," the young man said,
  "And are fat and uncommonly stout—
Why don't you eat yogurt and lettuce instead
  Of the treats that the children leave out?"

"In my youth," Father Christmas replied to the boy,
  "I was slim and got cold in a storm,
But now I eat only the food I enjoy,
  And now I stay perfectly warm."

"You are old, Father Christmas," the young man said,
  "And fat, yet uncommonly cute;
So why wear a hat of ridiculous red
  And model a tasteless red suit?"

"In my youth," Father Christmas replied to the wight,
  "I dressed in a becoming green,
But I got ran over one dark Christmas night,
  And since then I dress to be seen."

"You are old," Father Christmas," the young man said,
  "And fatter with each passing year,
Yet you ride through the sky in a rickety sled—
  Is not gravity something to fear?"

"In my youth," Father Christmas replied to the youth,
  "I'd never put up with such noise.
I've answered three questions with kindness and truth—
  Now be off, or I'll give you no toys!"

Give Presents to Your Little Boy

Give presents to your little boy,
   But break all those that please 'im,
And only do it to annoy
   Because you love to tease 'im.

        Ho! ho! ho!

I give good presents to my boy,
   I break all those that please 'im;
For he can thoroughly enjoy
   The sadist way I seize 'em.

        Ho! ho! ho!

Yalewocky

'Twas Christmas, and the Santa Claus
   Did jangle and jingle his bell;
All public-minded was his cause,
   With secrets none could tell.

"Beware the chilliness, my son,
   The frosts that bite, the colds that catch;
Beware the scrooginess, and shun
   The grinch's present-snatch."

He took his icicle in hand.
   Long time St. Nicolas he sought;
Then rested he by the Christmas tree
   And paced awhile in thought.

And as in greedy thought he'd pace,
   St. Nicholas with eyes of joy
Came flying through the fireplace
   And held a Christmas toy.

One, two! One, two! And through and through
   He rifled through Nicholas' sack;
And he did lift another's gift
   And would not give it back.

"And hast thou stole another's gift?
   Come to my whip, my thieving lad;
O Christmas day! Calloo! Callay!
   How could you be so bad?"

'Twas Christmas, and the Santa Claus
   Did jangle and jingle his bell;
All public-minded was his cause,
   With secrets none could tell.

To the Christmas-Eve World

To the Christmas-Eve world it was Santa that said,
"I've a present in hand and a hat on my head.
Let the Christmas-Eve creatures, wherever they be,
Not stir with my reindeer and elves dear and me!"

    Then fill up the stockings as quick as you can,
    And sprinkle the cookies with chocolate and bran:
    Put cake in the cocoa and toast in the tea—
    And welcome old Santa with thirty-times-three!

"O Christmas-Eve creatures," quoth Santa, "be still!
I've a tattle to tell and a stocking to fill.
'Tis a privilege high to find under the tree
A gift from my reindeer and elves dear and me!"

    Then fill up the stockings with snow-cones and meat
    Or anything else that is pleasant to eat:
    Mix owls with the oxen and cats with the kine—
    And welcome old Santa with ninety-times-nine!

The Mad Caroler's Song

He thought he saw a plate of ham
    To cause his stomach strife:
He looked again and found it was
    A present from his wife.
"If it is only cheese," he said,
    "I'll use my pocket knife!"

He thought he saw a Christmas tree
    Lighted for Halloween:
He looked again and found it was
    A rag with which to clean.
"The one thing I regret," he said,
    "Is that it is not green!"

He thought he saw a snowman dance
    Beneath a magic hat:
He looked again and found it was
    A grinning Cheshire cat.
"If this should melt away," he said,
    "The mouse will stir, not scat!"

He thought he saw a Santa Claus
    Ringing a silver bell:
He looked again and found it was
    A wooden wishing well.
"Were I to give a coin," he said,
    "There's nobody to tell!"

He thought he saw a maiden fair
    Beneath the mistletoe:
He looked again and found it was
    Some wild oats to sow.
"A kiss is but a kiss," he said,
    "And yet I'll tell her no!"

He thought he saw three sailing ships
    That shared a single hold:
He looked again and found it was
    A man ninety years old.
"You'd best be getting home," he said,
    "The nights are very cold!"

He thought he saw a rotund saint
    Out from the chimney fall:
He looked again and found it was
    An India rubber ball.
"It's big and red indeed," he said,
    "But brings no gifts at all!"

He thought he saw an argument
    That Plato might propose:
He looked again and found it was
    A reindeer's glowing nose.
"Should that prove bright indeed," he said,
    "To go it only shows!"

APPENDIX TWO

CELTIC CHRISTMAS CAROLS

We Sing Nowell

after the Breton "Kanomp Nowell"

Sing we nowell, nowell, nowell,
for Jesus Christ with us does dwell: we sing nowell.

O my brothers, we are here
with a song for our Lord to hear: we sing nowell.

Like tonight, that night gave birth
to the Savior of the earth: we sing nowell.

Joseph and Mary went forth
and they crisscrossed the whole earth: we sing nowell.

Sweating, stumbling, loss of breath
made this jouney worse than death: we sing nowell.

The Tree of Life

after the Cornish "A Das Ker My A Welas"

"O dear father, in God's place
I have seen a fount of grace
and beside it a tree grows.
A baby in napkins dressed
finds his high and holy rest
in the middle of its boughs."

It is God's own son you saw,
simply wrapped lest he be raw,
come to redeem Adam's debt
with his body and his blood.
Mother Mary, people good,
he will save when time is right.

Heavenly Father God is one,
and one is his only Son
whom a virgin shall give birth,
and the Spirit one must be—
three in one and one in three—
in this Godhead is my faith.

Jesus Christ the Lord is such
none can thank him overmuch
for carrying us to this place.
Let the time be ever stayed
when he was born of a maid,
of the virgin full of grace.

The Flight into Egypt

after the Irish Gaelic "An Teicheadh Go hÉigipt"

How weak was Herod when came unto his hearing
    the news of a king born better than he
in honor, lordship, in strength and in esteem.
    Deep anger and hatred filled his green heart.
           Pitiful!

But soon an angel appeared unto the virgin
    and said, "Flee to Egypt as quick as you can,
or soon you will hear wickedness without equal,
    and treachery and injustice and hate."
           Pitiful!

The three of them walked through the nocturnal darkness,
    the saint and the maid and the king of kings,
with nothing—no friendship, provisions or wealth:
    the king of heaven, and purity's babe.
           Pitiful!

Baby in Bethlehem

after the Manx "Oikan ayns Bethlehem"

Commemorate this holy day
   with purity within,
and celebrate Jesus the Christ,
   Baby in Bethlehem.

He left his Father's paradise
   and became human,
born of a virgin's purity,
   Baby in Bethlehem.

The angels of heaven rejoiced
   and came heavy-laden
with joy about a Savior born,
   Baby in Bethlehem.

Great is the meekness of the love
   that the lamb had within
who took the form of servanthood,
   Baby in Bethlehem.

Glory to God who gladly reigns
   from his throne in heaven,
and pours his goodwill unto earth,
   Baby in Bethlehem.

Blessed Child

after the Scottish Gaelic "Leanabh an Àigh"

Blessed sweet child, sweet Mary's child,
  born in a stable, elements' king,
down in this desert, suffering for us,
  blessed are those who chase after him.

Worldly rulers all have their children
  greatly rejoicing, great in their pomp.
Short is their lifespan, weak are their bodies,
  quickly their beauty fades in the grave.

Lamb who rescued us has no equal,
  modestly born and humbly begun.
Whole, undefiled maker of mankind
  rose from the dead and shattered the grave.

Prophets and seers, cherubs and seraphs
  spoke the desire giving them pulse;
wondrous and worthy of our devotion,
  blessed are those who chase after him.

Christ Child's Lullaby

after the Scottish Gaelic "Tàladh Chriosda"

My love, my dear, my darling true,
my only joy, my treasure new,
my beautiful, fair son are you.
   I don't deserve you near.
Alleluia, Alleluia,
Alleluia, Alleluia.

My precious darling from above,
my darling whose heart's filled with love,
gentle and helpless as a dove,
   great triumphs shall be yours.
Alleluia, Alleluia,
Alleluia, Alleluia.

You are the white sun in the sky.
Darkness will flee when you are nigh.
You will make sorrows from us fly
   and bring us holy light.
Alleluia, Alleluia,
Alleluia, Alleluia.

Behold! the Best of Mornings Dawns

after the Welsh "Wel, Dyma'r Borau Gorau I Gyd"

Behold! the best of mornings dawns
  full of delight and terror.
The light of Jesus Christ now shines
  and burns away our error.
The light of Jesus burns, and yet
  is loving, fresh and gentle.
This is the dawn he dons our flesh,
  and thus becomes a mortal.
The Son of God is sucking Mary's tits—
O eternal wonder! Oh, what singing fits
  these facts the Holy Spirit gives us!
Comforter, give each holy talent angel wings!
Believing souls care not when ancient aubade sings,
  but love to see the face of Jesus.

Free love poured out on humankind,
  grace from the heart of heaven,
ordained that through the Trinity
  blood sacrifice be given,
and that a Great One die to save
  all dwellers in the dust.
When the serpent begged us to eat,
  we broke God's law and trust.
In Eden—that tremendous paradise—we fell
like leaves, from linked to heaven to now linked to hell.
  Though to the depth of death we've fallen,
there is a Savior will raise us from lowiness
to the very heights of heavenly holiness—
  a loving, fresh and gentle lambkin.

Sing, Christians

after the Welsh "O Deued Pob Cristion"

Sing, Christians, who savor
the gift of God's favor
above every gift given men,
and your voices heighten
as angels enlighten,
since Bethlehem makes our hearts yen.

The king of the world
from heaven was hurled,
a savior to save us from sin:
all seekers are able
to find in a stable
a king never found in an inn.

To Mary the bearer
of Godhead (none fairer
in grace or in graces) now nod;
and kneel to no other
than him whom that mother
gave birth to, for he is our God.